Instructions in Madame Herman's New Method of Making Wax Flowers

Sarah E. Herman

ShapeBookStore reprints public domain books!

Visit us at http://www.shapebookstore.com

INSTRUCTIONS

IN

MADAME HERMAN'S

NEW METHOD OF

Making Wax Flowers,

WITH PRACTICAL ILLUSTRATIONS.

The same method which has been taught so successfully in New York to all her pupils in three hours' time.

First Edition.

This Book and an entire Set of Moulds may be had for $2.50, *from the author's address,*

MADAME HERMAN,

113 West 41st Street, New York City,

Who will be happy to explain anything which would not be generally understood.

Entered according to Act of Congress, in the year 1873, by MADAME HERMAN, in the Office of the Librarian of Congress, at Washington, D. C.

CONTENTS.

PREFACE.

Being convinced that the present book of instruction in my new method of making wax flowers would be acceptable to my pupils and others who wish to become acquainted with this beautiful art, has induced me to publish the following chapters.

This book has been made more particularly to supply the wants of persons living at a distance, and who can not come to this city to learn this method.

Any one with the "love of the beautiful" can not but admire well-made wax flowers which resemble nature so well that many persons are daily deceived by them, mistaking them for natural flowers; they are well adapted to decorative purposes, and nothing is more pretty for presents than wax flowers.

Careful attention to my course of lessons with the various plates accompanying them, will enable any one to learn my method in less hours than it takes to learn the old way in as many weeks.

The expense of the materials used being so little that it enables everybody to learn it, and will be appreciated by a look at my price list, giving the best quality of everything used, at a much smaller price than can be had from any wax-flower artist's place.

GENERAL REMARKS.

As all the flowers made by this method are made of melted cake-wax, it requires a lamp to melt the wax; the lamp I use is well adapted to that purpose; it is a small tin lamp put on the table, and burning alcohol; it has one or two burners, according to the size.

A few tin cups are necessary. They may be had from any tin shop at a cost of about 5 cents each; four or five of these will be sufficient.

The white cake-wax must be put into the tin cups, say 1 or $1\frac{1}{2}$ cakes in each. For white flowers, no colors or preparations are necessary, as the wax, when melted, will be beautifully white, if the pupil is careful not to let it boil.

Never let your wax boil, as it spoils it. When all the wax in the cup is melted, it is ready for use, and must be taken off the lamp, and when it gets cool, put it again on the lamp.

The sheet-wax is necessary for green and Fall leaves, and also for the yellow centres of Pond Lilies. The green sheet-wax is also used for covering stem wires.

The colors used are all marked in the price list, and are in small bottles. The various colors are scattered in the different cups, thus coloring the wax. It requires about one-third of a bottle for coloring a tin cup full of wax.

The most necessary cups of colored wax are:

A cup of rose colored wax for roses;

A cup of yellow colored wax for tea roses, centres of tuberoses, etc.

A cup of pure wax for all white flowers, and

A cup of green wax for several purposes.

The other colors are used dry with a small brush.

The Kremitz white is used for making a beautiful azure of the Prussian blue, and otherwise to make all colors lighter.

Mixing Burnt Umber with any color makes the said color darker.

Stamens are the centres of Morning Glories, Fuschias, etc., and are of different colors. Only six varieties are required.

Stem-wire is used for the stems of all flowers, and is already cut and put in packages of one ounce; they must be covered with strips of green sheet-wax; a little practice will be found necessary to cover the wires quickly.

Spool-wire is useful for the stems of green and autumn leaves; it is much thinner than stem-wire, and is covered with green cotton.

CHAPTER I.

NAMES OF THE MOULDS AND HOW TO USE THEM.

FIGURES 1, 2, 3 and 4 are the moulds used for the Pond Lily.

Figs. 5 and 6 are for making Roses.

Fig. 7 is the Morning Glory mould.

Fig. 8 is the Carnation Pink mould.

Fig. 9 is the Lily of the Valley mould.

The moulds must be put into a cup of cold water and remain there about five minutes before using.

They must be out of the water when not in use.

Every mould is used by dipping it into the hot wax and taking it out instantly.

Taking, for instance, the smallest Pond Lily mould (Fig. 1), by the wire, you dip it into the hot wax, and in taking it out instantly, you turn it, so that the drop of wax which otherwise would remain on the middle of the leaf goes to the end of it. Then you place it into the palm of your left hand and slide it gently, so that the hot wax (already cool) will remain in your left hand apart from the mould. Fig. 10 shows the way to take the wax off the mould; thus making a small Pond Lily leaf.

Before making another leaf, you must dip the mould into the cold water to prevent the wax from sticking to the mould.

Be careful not to let any drop of water fall into your hot wax.

PLATE I.

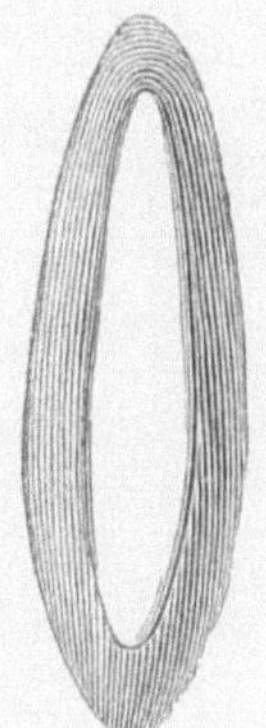

Fig. 1.

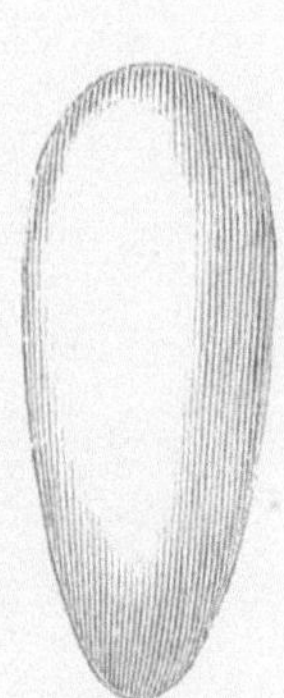

Fig. 2.

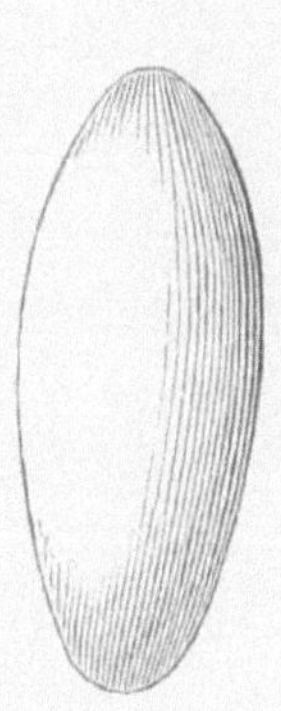

Fig. 3.

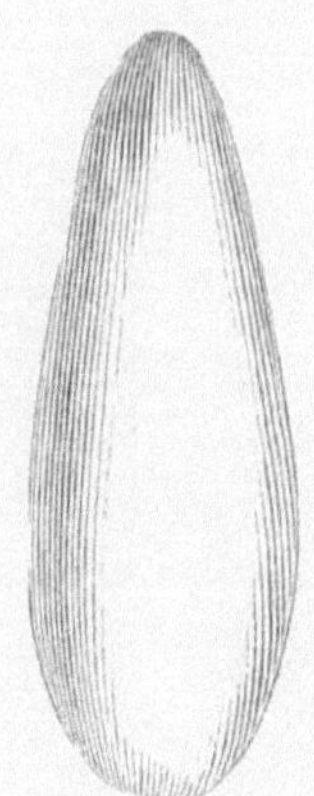

Fig. 4.

Fig. 5.

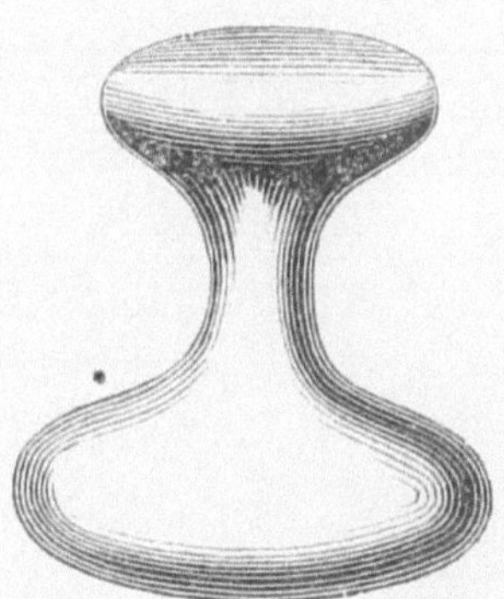

Fig. 6.

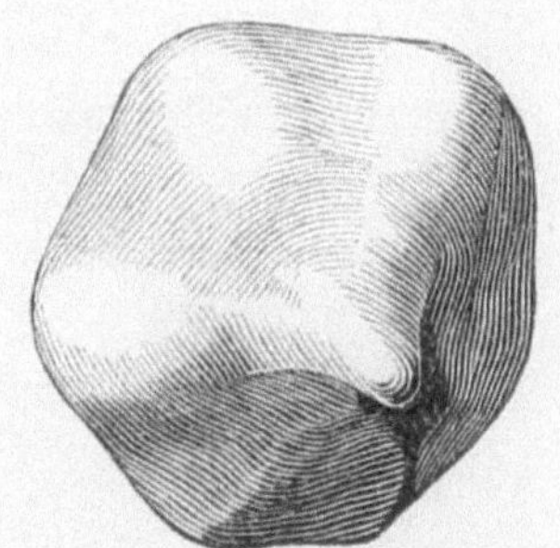

Fig. 7.

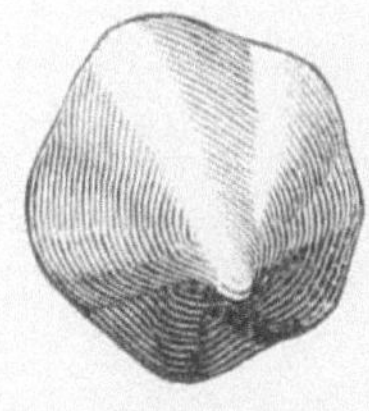

Fig. 8.

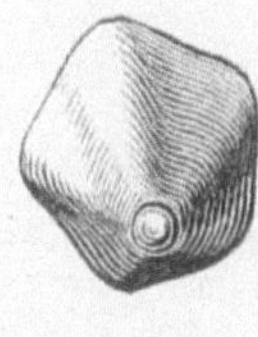

Fig. 9.

The Rose moulds are used in the same way, always being careful to turn them on one side in taking them out of the hot wax, to have the drop of wax go to the bottom of the leaf, thus making it perfect.

The Morning Glory mould is dipped into the wax and taken out perpendicularly, then the drop of wax will remain at the tip end of it. The best way to remove the wax from that mould is to transfer it into the left hand and put the thumb and two first fingers of the right hand round the mould and press the wax gently all around till it comes apart from the mould, as shown in Fig. 11.

A little practice will soon give the student the idea of the best way to remove the wax from the mould.

Do not dip more than three parts of the mould into the wax.

The Carnation Pink mould is used exactly as the Morning Glory mould; and so is the mould for the Lily of the Valley, with the exception that less than the fourth part of this last mould is dipped into the cup of hot wax.

CHAPTER II.

THE ROSE AND BUD.

MAKE a small hook at the end of one stem wire, and then cover it with green sheet-wax. The hook is necessary to prevent the Rose leaves from slipping in pressing them together. Then dip the small Rose mould (Fig. 5), into the wax, and thus make a small Rose leaf; the next thing is to place that leaf upon the stem; for that purpose you hold your covered wire with the left hand near the hook, and place the leaf upon that part of the stem, being careful to stick on the stem that part of the leaf where the drop of wax is, and you will find that the wax is so thoroughly adhesive that it requires but to press it gently on the stem to make it stick well; when your leaf is thus placed on the stem, you close it in rolling it around the stem in order to hide it and give a more natural shape to the flower. The wax is so pliable that you will experience no difficulty in giving to the leaves that shape which is so desirable, to avoid stiffness.

You proceed by dipping the same mould in the water; then make the second leaf and stick it in the same manner on the stem, but avoid closing it as much as the first leaf. Fig. 12 will show where to place this second leaf, thus illustrating the way of putting them together.

You continue in the same manner till you have made about three leaves more from this same small mould, making altogether five leaves; then you proceed with the second sized mould, which is the smaller end of mould Fig.

PLATE II.

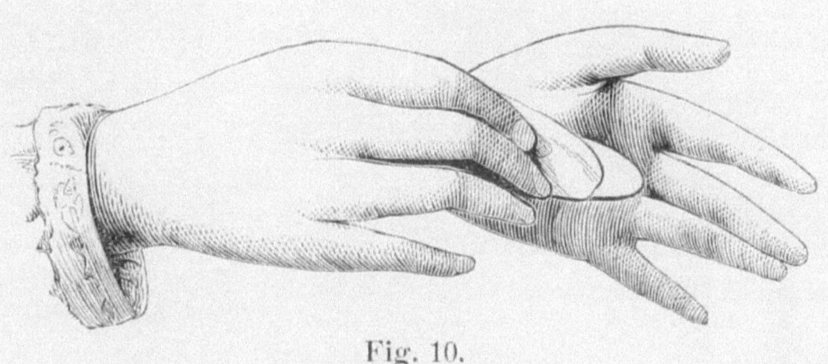

Fig. 10.

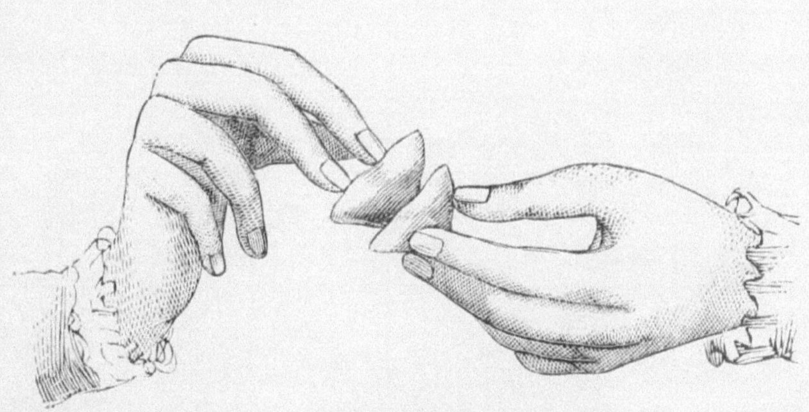

Fig. 11.

6, and make about the same quantity of leaves as you have done from the first mould, and so on with the third and fourth sizes—making altogether about twenty leaves.

It is better to have less, than more than that quantity of leaves to form the Rose.

If you wish to have a full-blown Rose, you alter the arrangement of one or two leaves made from the largest mould, in this way: instead of putting the hollow of the leaf over the other leaves as you have done throughout the Rose, you put the hollow outside, and it will look exactly as if that leaf would fall.

To finish the Rose, it requires now but the calyx, which is formed from the green sheet-wax. See Fig. 13 for the arrangement.

A half-blown bud is made exactly as the Rose, but from the two first moulds only, and finished with the calyx. See Fig. 13.

The closed bud is made in the following manner: You place on your wire a small Rose leaf as for the Rose, and taking your first sized mould, you dip about one third of *the side* of it into the hot wax—that is to say that instead of dipping the mould flat, you dip it on the side, thus making a kind of shell. You make four of these shells and place them around the first leaf, which is already on the stem. Fig. 13 shows this closed Rose bud. For making the green leaves, read Chapter XI, page 25.

ROSE.

Sweet Rose, when summer sunbeams play
  On lovely flowers on every side,
Thou, then the gayest of the gay,
  Blushest, the garden's fairest pride.

And though when summer days are o'er,
  (Alas, that lovely things should fade)
Thy beauty and thy blush no more
  Are in our gay parteres displayed.

Yet then, the fall'n and wither'd leaves
  Retain their well known rich perfume;
And e'en a faded rose-bud gives
  An useful moral from its tomb.

The fairest form must fade; but worth
  Will still survive though beauty dies;
When beauty stoops to kindred earth.
  Virtue immortal seeks the skies.

PLATE III.

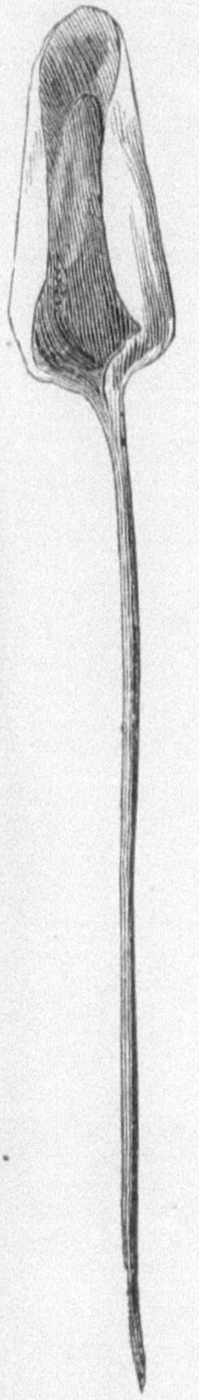

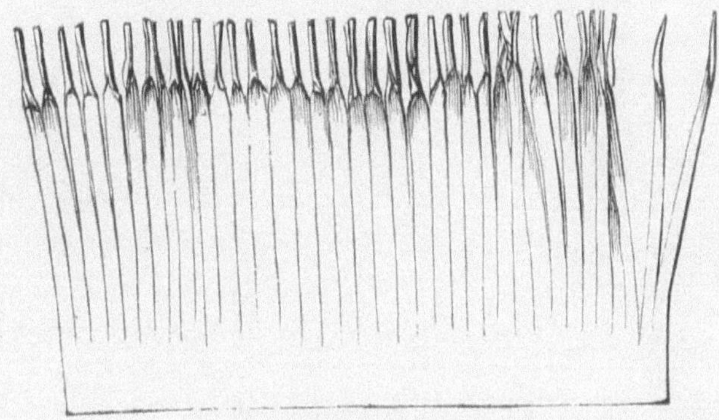

Fig. 14.

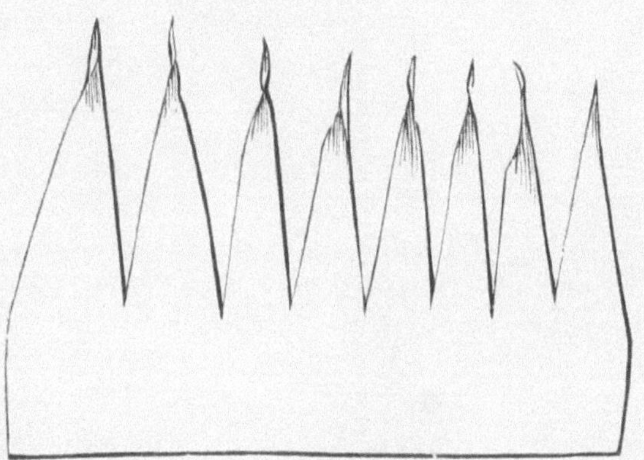

Fig. 15.

Fig. 12.

CHAPTER III.

THE POND OR WATER LILY.

An extensive locality of this plant exists upon the Saratoga Lake; its surface, for a quarter of a mile, may be seen whitened by these lilies, occasionally intermixed with the yellow lilies, and the rich blue of the Pontederia, another beautiful aquatic plant.

This beautiful flower may be imitated with great exactness. I shall choose for this chapter the common Lily of our rivers, as being the best known.

An extra thick wire for the stem is necessary, or two ordinary ones put together and covered over with green sheet-wax will do as well. Do not forget to make a small hook at the upper end of the wire to prevent the leaves from slipping upward in putting them together.

For the centre of the Lily, you must have yellow and orange sheet-wax. You take an ordinary sheet of yellow wax and divide the length into three parts; put one of these parts into your left hand, and with a pair of scissors cut strips as shown in Fig 14, and then pinch the top of each strip with the thumb and first finger; roll this around the stem from the base of those strips. When placed upon the stem, press the centre with the palm of your hand, to form a kind of ball, to imitate the natural centre of the Lily.

You proceed by taking the same quantity of orange sheet-wax and indent it with your scissors as shown in Fig. 15, and after having pinched the ends, you place this around the yellow centre, allowing the orange points to stand erect.

Then take your first mould, Fig. 1, by the wire, and dip it in the hot white wax, taking it out instantly, being careful to turn it with the larger end downward, to have the drop go there.

Be careful, also, not to dip this mould over the flat part of it, as it would make the leaf too large.

You place this first leaf on the wire and over the centre by cementing it with that end of the leaf where the drop of wax is; make another small leaf and place it *opposite* the first one in the same way; then a third and a fourth between the two first ones, and make four more leaves from the same first sized mould, thus making eight small pointed leaves.

Never make a new leaf until you are quite sure that you have cemented the others well on the stem.

After this, you take the second sized mould and make eight more leaves from it, being careful to let the drop of wax run to the smallest end of the mould; the top of the leaves will then be round, in contrast with the other leaves, which are pointed. Dip about a third of your mould into the hot wax.

Make eight more leaves from mould No. 3, and let the drop of wax run to the round part; then make eight more leaves from the largest mould, letting the drop of wax run to the round part, so that the leaves from the two last moulds will be pointed at the top.

The four leaves for the calyx are made from the largest mould, dipping it first in the white and then in the green hot wax.

Mix a small quantity of Burnt Umber with the same amount of Carmine, and rub it on the outside of the four leaves making the calyx.

The two colors thus mixed will be found useful also for the Pond Lily pads or leaves.

PLATE IV.

Fig. 13.

The bud is made with the same centre, and with sixteen leaves from the two first sized moulds, and the four leaves for the calyx are made from the second sized mould, thus making them round at the top.

Paint the calyx of the bud in the same manner as for the flowers.

CHAPTER IV.

THE LILY OF THE VALLEY.

THIS graceful little flower is made from mould No. 9. You dip a very small portion of this mould in the white wax; dip to the ridge part of the mould; make about eight of these coatings of wax; then cut the same quantity of spool-wire, about 1½ inch long, and another piece of spool-wire, about three inches long, for the stalk, and dip the top of the eight small wires into hot yellow wax, taking them out quickly, thus making very small balls of wax. This will imitate the pollen; and, to put it into the interior of the flower, it is best to make a small hole with a heated wire in the centre of the flower, and to pass the small wire with the pollen into it. Draw it tight, so that the small yellow ball touches the interior of the flower; cover the stem with green wax. The buds are best imitated by rolling some yellow wax around the top of the stems, and dipping into white wax. You then take each bell-like flower apart, and pinch four sides, which will prevent the bells from being quite so open.

This being done lightly, it will resemble much the natural flower; these will now require arranging on the long stalk, one of the smallest buds at the top, the rest following on either side, imitating, of course, the arrangement observable in the natural flower.

The student will notice that this requires now but the green leaves, which are long and narrow, and are made as explained in Chapter XI.

LILY OF THE VALLEY.

O, what a lovely moral tells,
The lily with its silver bells,
'Tis said they ring on summer nights,
Summoning all the fairy sprites,
To meet their tiny king and queen,
Under the oak or on the green.
If so, it surely is to bless—
How could the lily call to less?
To us of duller sense 'tis mute,
Yet eloquent as poet's lute.

Low in the vale retired it lies
Shunning the gaze of vagrant eyes;
Close to its own dear parent earth
It clings, the type of modest worth,
But hidden, though, in hood of green,
Too beautiful to be unseen;
Oft is it sought by those who prize
The modesty which fools despise;
Oft is it found by the proud few,
Who can esteem its virgin hue,
And leave the flowers of gaudier dye,
O'er the sweet valley flower to sigh.

Oh, is not this a happier fate
Than one short hour of pride elate;
Than one bright, gaudy, sunny day,
In blue and scarlet, and away—
Some may admire, but few can prize
The flaunting flowers of many dyes,
But all will seek the gentle one
Which seems the general gaze to shun;
Nor breathes its sigh of fragrance sweet
But to her lover at her feet.

Maidens, scorn not this humble tale
Of the sweet Lily of the Vale.

CHAPTER V.

THE MORNING GLORY.

THE Convolvulus, or Morning Glory, is made from mould No. 7, by dipping three parts of it into white wax, and removing as shown in Fig. 11.

You then color your Morning Glory with a brush dipped in dry paint, though I prefer to rub it on with the first finger.

Some Morning Glories have narrow colored stripes, and others are colored nearly all over. The colors most observable in Morning Glories are blue, purple and pink.

Take a long piece of spool-wire and fasten to one end of it, with a little piece of wax, four stamens folded in the middle, and one not folded, thus making eight heads of stamens together, and one single head, longer than the others. The color of the stamens must be according to the color of the flower.

Having made a small hole through your Morning Glory, you pass the spool-wire through, and draw it tight from the outside, so that the stamens remain stationary in the centre. You then fix four small calyx, and, taking an ordinary pencil, you twist the wire around it, and the flower is made.

A spray of Morning Glories, of different colors, interwoven with ivy leaves and Morning Glory leaves, looks very pretty around rustic baskets, etc.

IVY CONVOLVULUS.

Where stocks and harebells blossoming,
  Shed fragrance o'er a flow'ry bed;
A sapling of the last year's spring
  Weaved to the wind its feeble head.

And oft it dropped a tear, as though
  It wept, because it upward grew,
And bent a frequent look below,
  As loth to bid the sweets adieu.

But flowers will fade, and one by one
  Did each its scent or beauty lose;
Now where the rose's blushes gone,
  And faded now the tulip's hues.

Fair, fragile, and inconstant friends;
  A summer pair, they all were gone;
And as the oak tree upward tends,
  It stands deserted and alone.

And so had liv'd, and so decay'd,
  But, springing from its wither'd bough,
An Ivy spread its mantling shade,
  And bursting, blossoms o'er it now.

And the two friends so closely twine,
  The tree supports—the flower adorns;
The oak need not for youth repine,
  Nor the frail Ivy fear the storms.

And thus should friendship ever be
  Founded on qualities which last,
That it may live on sympathy,
  When beauty and youth are past.

CHAPTER VI.

THE DARK CLOVE PINK.

THIS dark, rich-colored flower may be easily imitated, and is most effective in contrast with other most delicate-tinted flowers.

It is made with mould No. 8, by dipping the three-quarters of it into white wax, and removed from the mould as shown in Fig. 11. Make four of these coatings.

A rather ragged or serrated edge must be given with the scissors, and when thus clipped all around, cut it right through on one side, that is to say, cut from the edge to the bottom of the bell on one side only, and cut the three other coatings in the same manner. You then proceed by coloring the coatings with Carmine on both sides with a small brush or finger.

Or you may obtain this color by squeezing some carmine oil paint into a cup of white wax and make the coatings from it.

For the foundation, take a piece of stem-wire, covered with green sheet-wax, and, on this, place the two anthers, or horns, cut from white paper and dipped into white wax; then place the four petals around this, bending them backward, and avoiding anything approaching stiffness in the arrangement.

After the petals are placed on, make the seed-cup; for this you take an ordinary pencil, and having scraped the color with a knife about three-fourths of an inch, you let it soak in water for a few minutes, and having melted some green wax, but not too warm, as it would make the seed-cup too thin, you dip your pencil in it and take it out quickly; if it is still too thin you dip it once more in the wax which will make two coatings one over the other, and having removed from the pencil, you cut them with the scissors to make the four various parts of the calyx.

Almost any shade, from scarlet to deep purple, is found in these flowers, and all may be, with a little care, easily produced.

If you wish to make a varegated pink, you make the petals from white wax, and when clipped all around, you color, with a small brush, a few stripes, very narrow, on each petal with carmine, and finish as explained for the clove carnation.

CHAPTER VII.

The Tuberose.

The Tuberose is best imitated from the smallest Pond Lily mould. Having covered your wire with your sheet wax, you roll some white wax around the top of it, thus making a kind of ball to imitate the pollen, and proceed by making the petals from the small pond lily mould dipped in white wax.

Place these petals around the pollen. The outside leaves must be gracefully bent backward and a little curled.

You finish it by dipping the part cemented on the stem very slightly in hot green wax, to make a kind of calyx.

This flower is very nice in a boquet, its whiteness must be perfect.

TUBEROSE.

First fair floweret of the year,
  'Mid thy white and savory bed,
Welcome spring's first harbinger,
  Gold-tip Tuberose, rear thy head.

Not the nipping northern fear,
  Let not frost or snow alarm;
Through the wintry waste appear;
  I will shelter thee from harm.

Happy harbinger of spring,
  See appear its golden rays;
And, sweet floweret, seems to bring
  Hopes of warmer, brighter days.

And so we often find there is,
  E'en in hours of deepest care,
Sweet forerunning hopes of bliss,
  Warning, guarding from despair.

CHAPTER VIII.

The White Camelia.

This beautiful flower can be well imitated by using the rose moulds. You firstly roll some white wax around the stem, making a small ball as large as the end of the little finger, and then dip it into the cup of hot white wax, to make it perfectly pure. Then make four small leaves from the first sized rose mould, and place them around this ball, but rather low, so that they do not go over the ball more than a third of an inch. Make four more leaves from the same mould, and in placing them on the stem you must draw them backward in holding the fastening part of each leaf firmly over the stem with your left hand, so that it does not come apart from the stem; those few leaves must be drawn down from the edge till they are almost in a horizontal line, then take the second sized mould and make four more leaves from it, and place them horizontally as the others, and continue with the two largest moulds in making four leaves from each. Then finish by making a very small calyx, and make a spray of green leaves. It is very important to have perfectly pure wax for this flower.

CHAPTER IX.

THE FUSCHIA.

THE Fuschia is made from the smallest rose mould and the smallest pond lily mould. You take a piece of spool wire and fasten to one end of it eight stamens and one longer than the rest, as for the morning glory; then make the four petals of the corolla from the small rose mould, in dipping only one half of the flat part in white wax, place those eight leaves gracefully around the stamens. The four sepals of calyx are made from the small pond lily mould, by dipping in the white wax the flat part of it only; place these around the petals.

To finish with the body of the flower, you dip the pencil as for the pink's seed-cup, but into white wax, about half an inch; pass the wire through it, it will then hide that part of the flower where the sepals are fastened to the wire; give a nice curve to those sepals. Dip in green wax the top of the body to make the small seed-cup.

Fuschias are of many different colors. A very delicate one is the petals or centre being white, and the four sepals and body pink madder; they must be painted before placed on the stem with a small brush or finger; give a delicate shade of green to the points.

Some others have a crimson centre and white outside leaves.

Others have a beautiful purple centre and crimson outside.

The bud is made on the same kind of wire as the flower, without any stamens; the centre may be omitted as it would be covered over by the outside leaves which meet at the points, thus hiding the interior.

A nice spray can be made with the green leaves on an extra strong and long wire, covered with green sheet wax, and to the end of it you attach the two smallest buds and the two smallest leaves, you may secure them on the large stem with a very fine piece of thread, covered over with green sheet wax till the junction of the next two leaves; then two more buds or flowers, and so on; the buds always at the top of the spray.

FUSCHIA.

Beside the rosy bower of love,
  Blest with the smile of sunny skies,
With sweets around it and above,
The drooping Fuschia poured its sighs.

For the gay summer time had passed,
  And brought no blossom to its bough;
And Autumn plucked, with envious haste,
  The fading flowers from his brow.

"O will the waning year pass by,
  Scattering on all around one bloom,
While I unblest, unfavored die,
  No blush, no blossom, no perfume.

While ever bounteous nature showers
  Its rainbow loveliness around;
And e'en the wreck of summer flowers
  Strews with gay beauty the rich ground.

Must I, poor unimpassioned flower,
  Thus coldly live, and nun-like die,
Growing by Love's own rosy bower,
  Without one glance from his dear eye."

Just then flew by the wayward child,
  And thus the pensive Fuschia mourned,
And the capricious urchin smiled,
    As to the plant his arrow turned.

The bolt had scarcely left his bow,
  'Ere pendent pearls on each branch move,
Which, changed to his own tint, are now
  The emblems of "accepted love."

CHAPTER X.

The Sweet Pea.

This delicate flower is the easiest to make.

Make it on spool wire.

Make from the smallest rose mould and white wax three small leaves; cut the first one all around to make it about half the size from what it was before, cut the second one, to have it a little larger and leave the third one the full size, as taken from the mould, and proceed by coloring the two first ones with pink madder, the largest leaf remaining white. You then stick the smallest leaf on the stem and bring the edges together, which will make one sharp edge in front, then place the second leaf at the back of the first one and stick it on the wire, pinch it at the top, from the back, to curve that leaf inward, on each side of the first one.

You then place the third leaf on the stem at the back of the two first ones, with the hollow part backward in contrast with the others.

Finish it by adding four little pieces of sheet wax for the calyx.

Some sweet peas have the three leaves colored purple.

SWEET PEA.

My little fragile favorite, whither art thou tending?
Thy butterfly-like blossoms, why thus are they sporting?
Where are now thy pliant little tendrils wending;
Whither are they wandering, or what are they courting?

I have seen roses bloom—I too have seen lilies,
Primroses and cowslips, pinks and daffodillies;
Some excel in beauty, some enchant by meekness,
Little flower, they tell me thy charm is in thy weakness.

Even from thy birth, of flowers or plants the weakest,
Long ere thy blossoms burst, a firm support thou seekest;
And as around thy prop, thou thy small tendrils wreathest,
O, all the sweetness there, of thy fragrant soul thou breathest.

Sweet breath—sweet flower—sweet weakness, ever clinging
To the one chosen prop from the beginning—
O surely love is here! and though shadowed but in flowers,
Each breath, each slightest tint of "the all beautiful" is ours.

CHAPTER XI.

The Green and Autumn Leaves.

Brass moulds are indispensable to make those leaves.

Take for instance the rose leaf mould (brass) and dip it in cold water, then take a sheet of green wax and place it on the back of the mould, that is where the veins are most conspicuous; press the wax with the thumb on every part of the brass mould, then take a piece of spool wire and place it half way on the middle of the wax which is on the mould, then put another sheet of wax over the first one, covering of course the stem.

To have a well made leaf, it then requires to press well this second sheet of wax upon the first one, in order to take all the impressions of the brass mould; when this is done you press your thumb all around the sharp edge of the mould, this will separate all the wax around the mould.

The next thing is to remove the leaf (already made) from the mould. This will easily come apart by passing the thumb all around the edge.

Never use a brass mould without dipping it into cold water, as the wax would adhere to it.

Every leaf is made in the same manner. You need not take two sheets of green wax to make a leaf; after having put one part of a sheet over the mould and placed the wire on the ridge part of it, you then fold the other part of the sheet wax over it.

It is very important to press well those two sheets on the brass mould, as it will take a very good impression of every vein, and will also, when taken out of the mould, look much thinner than it would have done if not properly pressed over the mould.

In winter, the sheet wax is liable to become brittle, it can be softened by pressing it between the hands or passed over the fire.

The fall leaves are made in the same way, but when taken off the mould, are painted with carmine, yellow and brown, and sometimes blue.

A good way to produce the fall leaves is to make them out of yellow instead of green wax, and then to color them over.

There is some variegated sheet wax sold for autumn leaves, but I prefer them painted after they are made.

It is well to cover the stems of leaves with sheet wax to hide the cotton, though they can be covered from the hot green wax with a small brush.

The Pond Lily pad is generally glossy; after having painted it as explained in Chapter III, you brush it over the color with a brush, or rub it with the fleshy part of the hand, and you will obtain that shiny appearance.

CHAPTER XII.

Concluding Remarks.

If the wax is warmer than it should be, the coating on the mould will be too thin; and if too cool the coating will be thicker than is desirable. When too cold it should be put again over the lamp. The right heat is to be found only by practice.

Before using scissors to cut wax, always dip them in cold water.

If the sheet wax be too brittle, warm it between your hands, or over a fire.

I have found that a little silver white from the oil tube mixed with hot white wax gives that crisp whiteness to the Camelia which is so characteristic with that flower.

When your white wax becomes yellow or dirty, warm it over, and pour it over some other colored wax, as your white wax must always be perfectly pure.

When not in use, cover your cups with a piece of linen, or turn them over to prevent the dust from spoiling the wax.

Never waste any wax, all clippings can be melted in the green cup of wax.

For the mixing of the colors with the white wax, you scatter a small quantity of the color into the hot wax, and you stir it with a small brush, and then try if the color is right by dipping a mould in the wax, thus making a leaf; if you have put too much color into the wax, you add more wax to it, and if the color is too light you add more color to it.

PRICE LIST OF MATERIALS.

1 Small Lamp, one burner, - -	50c.	$0 00
1 Large " two " - - - - - - - -		1 00
1 Pound of Wax, - - - - - - -		85
1 Vial Chrome Green, 1 " " Yellow, 1 " Orange Chrome, 1 " Rose Madder, 1 " Carmine, No. 40 1 " Prussian Blue, 1 " French Purple, 1 " Burnt Umber, 1 " Kremitz White,	10c. each or the 9 bottles for	90

BRASS MOULDS FOR GREEN LEAVES.

3 Sizes Moulds for Roses, 2 " " Camelias, 2 " " Fuschias, 3 " " Pond Lilies, 2 " " Lilies of the Valley, 3 " " Ivy, 3 " " Geranium,	The doz.	1 00
3 Camel's Hair Brushes, 4c. each, - - - - -		12
4 Doz. Pale and Dark Green Sheet Wax 1 " Yellow Sheet Wax, 1 " Orange " "	6 dozen,	60
1 Oil Tube Silver White for Camelias, - - - -		15
1 Spool Wire, - - - - - - - - -		10
1 oz. Stem Wire, - - - - - - - - -		10
6 Bunches Stamens for - - - - - -		25
		$5 07

N. B. The above list of materials is what is required by

each student. The amount being $5.07 in having a large lamp, or $4.57 if a small lamp is required.

All those articles can be sent to any part of the United States, and may be paid on delivery, thus saving all trouble.

Orders promptly attended to.

Any article used for Wax Flowers always on hand.

www.ingramcontent.com/pod-product-compliance
Ingram Content Group UK Ltd.
Pitfield, Milton Keynes, MK11 3LW, UK
UKHW041905190726
13854UKWH00003B/1098

9 781300 261292